CORE LIBRARY OF US STATES

# COLORADO

**BY LAURA PERDEW**

**CONTENT CONSULTANT**
Derek Everett, PhD
Senior Instructor, Department of History
Colorado State University

Core Library
An Imprint of Abdo Publishing
abdobooks.com

**abdobooks.com**

Published by Abdo Publishing, a division of ABDO, PO Box 398166, Minneapolis, Minnesota 55439.


Printed in the United States of America, North Mankato, Minnesota.
052022
092022

THIS BOOK CONTAINS RECYCLED MATERIALS

Cover Photo: Shutterstock Images
Interior Photos: Sean Xu/Shutterstock Images, 4–5; Red Line Editorial, 9 (Colorado), 9 (USA); Shutterstock Images, 10–11, 17 (tree), 18, 32, 34–35, 40, 43; Zack Frank/Shutterstock Images, 13; Filip Bjorkman/Shutterstock Images, 17 (flag); Tom Reichner/Shutterstock Images, 17 (sheep); Images by Dr. Alan Lipkin/Shutterstock Images, 17 (flower); Danny Ye/Shutterstock Images, 17 (stegosaurus); Kevin Ruck/Shutterstock Images, 20–21, 45; Sandra Foyt/Shutterstock Images, 23; Universal History Archive/Universal Images Group/Getty Images, 26–27; Elena Arrigo/Shutterstock Images, 31; Dustin Bradford/Icon Sportswire/Getty Images, 39

Editor: Marie Pearson
Series Designer: Joshua Olson

**Library of Congress Control Number: 2021951380**

**Publisher's Cataloging-in-Publication Data**

Names: Perdew, Laura, author.
Title: Colorado / by Laura Perdew
Description: Minneapolis, Minnesota : Abdo Publishing, 2023 | Series: Core library of US states | Includes online resources and index.
Identifiers: ISBN 9781532197475 (lib. bdg.) | ISBN 9781098270230 (ebook)
Subjects: LCSH: U.S. states--Juvenile literature. | Western States (U.S.)--Juvenile literature. | Colorado--History--Juvenile literature. | Physical geography--United States--Juvenile literature.
Classification: DDC 978.8--dc23

Population demographics broken down by race and ethnicity come from the 2019 census estimate. Population totals come from the 2020 census.

# CONTENTS

CHAPTER ONE

# THE CENTENNIAL STATE

A car travels west on Trail Ridge Road in Rocky Mountain National Park. Fresh, warm summer air rushes in through the open windows. The car passes a wide-open meadow edged by forest. A herd of elk grazes in the middle. The car whooshes by tall ponderosa pines, with thick trunks and reddish bark, and aspen trees, with bright white bark. The road keeps winding uphill.

Eventually the trees give way to shrubs. Soon the road is in the tundra, where the

**Rocky Mountain National Park is full of spectacular views.**

## PERSPECTIVES

### WOMEN AND NATIONAL PARKS

Rocky Mountain National Park was dedicated on September 4, 1915. It was the nation's tenth national park. Mary Belle King Sherman, a leader of the National Federation of Women's Clubs, attended the dedication. Across the country these clubs had worked to make a national park in Colorado. Sherman believed that national parks were an important part of the health, education, and well-being of all Americans. She said, "Every community should have a place in which the people may spend their leisure time, where they will be brought in direct contact with things of beauty and interest in the outdoor world."

plants are only inches high. Even though it is summertime, the high mountain air is cold. The car reaches the highest point on the road at 12,183 feet (3,713 m) above sea level. This is where it crosses the Continental Divide. All rivers east of this divide flow into the Atlantic Ocean. Rivers to the west flow into the Pacific. From the mountaintop there are views in every direction of jagged peaks, rolling tundra, alpine lakes, and deep valleys.

## ABOUT COLORADO

Colorado's nickname is the Centennial State. It got this name because it became a state in 1876, 100 years after the Declaration of Independence was signed. A centennial is a 100th anniversary. Colorado is part of the western region of the United States. It is bordered by Wyoming to the north, Nebraska to the northeast, and Kansas to the east. Oklahoma and New Mexico are to the south, and Utah is to the west. The southwest corner of Colorado is the only place in the United States where four

### GETTING ITS NAME

The name Colorado has its origins in the Spanish word for "colored red." That was the name explorers from Spain gave to the Colorado River when they saw it in what is now the southern United States. The river has a reddish color due to the red sandstone soil of the area. The river starts in what is now the state of Colorado. So the name Colorado was given to the region in 1861 when it became a territory.

states meet. These states are Colorado, Utah, Arizona, and New Mexico.

Colorado is known for its Rocky Mountains and rushing rivers. Yet the eastern third of the state is plains. Cities in this area include Lamar and Sterling. Denver is the capital city of Colorado. It sits on the western edge of the plains at the base of the mountains. The area to the north and south of Denver is called the Front Range urban corridor. Several of Colorado's other major cities are on the Front Range urban corridor, including Fort Collins, Boulder, Colorado Springs, and Pueblo.

The Rocky Mountains lie west of Denver. There are many mountain towns, including Breckenridge and Steamboat Springs. Many of these towns are ski towns. In the west there are mountains, canyons, plateaus, deserts, and the Colorado River. The largest city in this part of the state is Grand Junction. Colorado is an amazing state to explore, featuring diverse beauty, wild history, and unique culture.

# MAP OF COLORADO

**Colorado is a state with a diverse landscape. What do you notice about the locations of many of the major cities?**

CHAPTER TWO

# HISTORY OF COLORADO

People lived on the land that is now Colorado more than 10,000 years ago. These prehistoric people, now called Paleo-Indians, crafted spears with arrowheads. They hunted bison and mammoths. In the 500s CE, Ancestral Puebloans settled in the Mesa Verde area. They developed a rich culture that included farming, making pottery, developing the bow and arrow, and building adobe dwellings. Some of these dwellings were built

People can see the remains of an Ancestral Puebloan cliff dwelling at Mesa Verde National Park.

into the sides of cliffs. Many are now preserved in Mesa Verde National Park.

Several American Indian nations have lived in what is now Colorado for hundreds of years. The Comanche (Nʉmʉnʉʉ), Apache, Cheyenne, and Arapaho peoples lived on the eastern plains. The Utes were one of the peoples living in the mountains.

## EUROPEANS ARRIVE

The Spanish were the first Europeans to reach Colorado. During one expedition in 1598, much of western Colorado was claimed for Spain, even though American Indians already lived there. This was the beginning of centuries of clashes between American Indian nations and settlers across Colorado. In 1682 French explorer Robert de La Salle claimed the land east of the mountains. This land became part of the Louisiana Territory. In 1803 the US government bought that land in the Louisiana Purchase.

Bent's Old Fort stands where the US-Mexico border once was.

The western land remained part of the Spanish territory until 1821. At that time Mexico gained its independence from Spain. Western Colorado came under Mexican rule. In 1846 the United States and Mexico went to war over the land. This was the Mexican-American War (1846–1848). The United States won the war and took control of western and southern Colorado. Mexicans continued living on the land.

## PATH TO STATEHOOD

Throughout the early 1800s, more white settlers moved to what is now Colorado. At first they were mostly trappers and fur traders. Then in the 1850s, gold was discovered in Colorado. This Colorado Gold Rush brought even more people to the state hoping to get rich. Others began farming and raising cattle to feed the local miners. It was a boom time for the area. In response to the population growth, the US government established the Colorado Territory in 1861. The new territory included land acquired during the Louisiana

### COLORADO FLAG

The Colorado state flag consists of three equally sized horizontal stripes of blue, white, and blue. The blue represents the blue skies of Colorado. The white is symbolic of the snow on the mountains. In the middle of the flag is a thick red C with a circle of yellow in the middle. The yellow circle recognizes the state's sunny weather as well as the gold mined there. And the red C represents Colorado's red sandstone soils.

Purchase and the Mexican-American War as well as from other territories.

The growth was not without cost. The clashes between settlers and American Indians continued. Settlers forced American Indians off the lands they had controlled for centuries. Treaties took away more than 90 percent of American Indian lands. Many American Indian leaders tried to bring peace between nations and settlers. These leaders included Chief Little Raven, a member of the Arapaho Nation. Despite these efforts, tensions grew in the mid-1800s. Then in 1864 the governor of Colorado blamed the murder of a white family on American Indians. This stirred settlers' fear and resentment of American Indians. Cheyenne and Arapaho leaders tried again to make peace. Instead the Colorado Cavalry attacked the Cheyenne and Arapaho settlement along Sand Creek southwest of Denver. Troops killed approximately 200 peaceful Cheyenne and Arapaho people. Troops burned the

## PERSPECTIVES

### HISPANIC AND LATINO HERITAGE

Colorado has a rich Hispanic and Latino heritage. People of Mexican ancestry have lived in southwestern Colorado since the 1600s. They were first under Spanish rule. Then Mexico won its independence from Spain in 1821. These same people came under Mexican rule. At the end of the Mexican American War, those Mexicans became US citizens. Today people with Mexican heritage are referred to as Mexican Americans. Latino refers to people with Latin American heritage. The word Hispanic applies to all people with Spanish language heritage, including those from Spain. In Colorado this is now a diverse community with a variety of languages and backgrounds.

village before leaving. The event became known as the Sand Creek Massacre.

As with American Indians, many Mexican settlers also had their land rights stripped away after the Mexican-American War. Some struggled to hold on to their land. Cases that went to court were often dismissed. US control over land in Colorado expanded.

## GOVERNMENT

Colorado became the thirty-eighth

## COLORADO
# QUICK FACTS

**Examine these facts and symbols of Colorado. Why do you think each is important to people in Colorado?**

**Abbreviation:** CO
**Nickname:** The Centennial State
**Motto:** *Nil sine numine* (Nothing without providence or deity)
**Date of statehood:** August 1, 1876
**Capital:** Denver
**Population:** 5,773,714
**Area:** 104,094 square miles (269,602 sq km)

## STATE SYMBOLS

**State animal**
Rocky Mountain bighorn sheep

**State fossil**
Stegosaurus

**State flower**
White-and-lavender columbine

**State tree**
Colorado blue spruce

Colorado's state government is based out of the Colorado State Capitol building.

state on August 1, 1876. Because of the diversity of people living in the state, the constitution was written in English, Spanish, and German. The state's citizens are represented in the legislative, executive, and judicial branches of the state government. The people of Colorado also have the right to introduce laws and amend the state's constitution.

Today there are only two federally recognized American Indian tribes in the state. They are the Ute Mountain Ute Tribe and the Southern Ute Indian Tribe. Both act separately from and independently of the state government.

# STRAIGHT TO THE SOURCE

Little Raven was born in 1810 on the plains. He grew up to become a chief of the southern Arapaho people. He worked to keep the peace between plains peoples and white settlers. Still, these settlers forced him and other American Indian peoples off their lands. Following the Sand Creek Massacre, he said:

> *It will be a very hard thing to leave the country that God gave us. Our friends are buried there, and we hate to leave these grounds. . . . That fool band of soldiers that cleared out our lodges and killed our women and children. This is hard on us. There at Sand Creek—White Antelope and many other chiefs lie there; our women and children lie there. Our lodges were destroyed there, and our horses were taken from us there, and I do not feel disposed to go right off to a new country and leave them.*

Source: Dee Brown. *Bury My Heart at Wounded Knee*. Sterling, 2001, p. 100. *Google Books*, books.google.com. Accessed 3 Aug. 2021.

## WHAT'S THE BIG IDEA?

Read the above quote carefully. What do Chief Little Raven's words say about his connection to the land and to his people? How was the move to a new land different for American Indians than for the white settlers moving west?

CHAPTER THREE

# GEOGRAPHY AND CLIMATE

Colorado is in the Rocky Mountain region, yet 40 percent of the state is flat. The geography varies from high plains to towering mountains to deserts. There are four regions in the state. The eastern plains are flat and gently slope upward toward the western mountains. The mountains in Colorado are part of the Rocky Mountains that extend from Canada to Mexico. The range runs through the middle of the state from north to south. In the mountains 54 peaks

People visit ski resorts in Colorado's mountains during the winter.

## PERSPECTIVES

### PALISADE PEACHES

**West of the mountains is a town called Palisade. In the summer Palisade has hot days and cool nights. This combination brings out a peach's natural sugars and helps it grow large. The result is big, sweet, juicy peaches. Because of this Palisade is known as the Peach Capital of Colorado. There's even a yearly festival celebrating peaches. The town's motto is, "Life tastes good here all year long."**

reach higher than 14,000 feet (4,270 m) above sea level. In addition, the Continental Divide runs through Colorado's mountains. Six major rivers, including the Rio Grande and the Colorado River, have their headwaters in the region.

The third region, the Colorado Plateau, is west of the mountains. This area is lower in elevation, with plateaus, mesas, hills, and valleys. Finally, the Intermontane Basin is in the northwest corner. It is the smallest region of the state. It has plateaus and rolling, forested hills.

People can enjoy scenic views by taking roads, including one across Loveland Pass, that cross the Continental Divide.

## CLIMATE

Colorado gets about 300 sunny days per year. Overall the climate is dry with low humidity. The state experiences four seasons. However, there are great differences in climate across the state. The eastern and western parts of the state are warmer than the central mountains. Because of Colorado's high elevation and low humidity, the temperatures across the state also vary greatly between day and night.

Snowfall totals are different by location too. Mountain towns can receive more than 15 feet (4.6 m) of snow in a year. On the other hand, Denver gets only about 4.5 feet (1.4 m) per year. Grand Junction gets less than 1.6 feet (0.5 m).

## NATIVE SPECIES RETURN

For thousands of years, American Indians lived and hunted in what is now Colorado. They hunted only what they needed. When European settlers arrived in the 1800s, that balance shifted. Settlers hunted both bison and lynx to extinction or near extinction in the state. More recently wildlife biologists have worked to return these species to Colorado. The lynx reintroduction in the mountains began in 1999. On the eastern plains, bison were returned in the early 2000s.

## PLANTS AND ANIMALS

Colorado has a great variety of plants and animals. The eastern plains are covered in prairie grasses. This region is home to pronghorn, coyotes, and prairie dogs. Tarantulas also live in southeastern Colorado. They can be seen leaving their burrows each September in search of mates. Eastern Colorado was also once home to large herds of bison. The herds in the West were almost wiped out in the 1800s due to overhunting by settlers.

Recent conservation efforts have brought bison back to the plains.

In the mountains there are aspen and pine trees such as the Colorado blue spruce. There are also many types of wildflowers, such as the state flower, the white-and-lavender columbine. Animals include bighorn sheep, mountain lions, lynx, marmots, elks, and hawks.

West of the mountains, the Colorado Plateau's plants consist mostly of arid grasses, sagebrush, and short junipers. Horned lizards, mule deer, jackrabbits, and pinyon jays all live on the Colorado Plateau.

## EXPLORE ONLINE

**Chapter Three discusses some of Colorado's plants and animals. The article at the website below has a page that describes more of the state's animals. What other Colorado species did you learn about from the website?**

### ANIMALS

**abdocorelibrary.com/colorado**

CHAPTER FOUR

# RESOURCES AND ECONOMY

Colorado has experienced economic booms and busts since even before its statehood. One of the first booms was in the fur trade in the 1830s and 1840s. But the fur trade caused animals to be overhunted. The number of animals dropped. At the same time, fashion trends changed. There was less demand for fur. By the 1850s the industry had experienced a bust.

The next boom followed the discovery of gold near present-day Denver in 1858.

People who came looking for gold were called prospectors.

During the Colorado Gold Rush, thousands of people moved to the area to strike it rich mining gold.

## THE RAILROAD

The discovery of gold in Colorado in 1858 increased the effort to bring railroads to Colorado. In 1870 the US railroad system finally reached Denver. It soon spread throughout the state, including into the mountains. To move through the winding mountain terrain, companies developed a railroad where the tracks were closer together. These narrow-gauge lines allowed trains to handle tight curves. They were also cheaper to build and more efficient than the standard rails. The new rail system helped with the export of metals out of the state. It also brought in tourists, goods, and residents.

A discovery of silver in the late 1870s led to another boom. Numerous towns and cities were established during these booms. Many, such as Leadville and Breckenridge, are still thriving. Others are ghost towns because the price of silver plummeted in the 1890s. Many mines closed. Businesses that supported the mines and workers also closed. Some towns were abandoned as thousands of workers left in search of jobs.

Despite the bust in the late 1800s, mining continues in the state today. The main products are coal, oil, and natural gas. Sand, gravel, gold, silver, copper, other metals, and rocks are also mined in the state. And after the mining bust, other industries such as agriculture and tourism grew.

## PERSPECTIVES

### 10TH MOUNTAIN DIVISION

Colorado's mountains provided a valuable training ground during World War II (1939–1945). Camp Hale was established in December 1942 in the Eagle River Valley. More than 11,000 troops trained there to prepare for combat in Europe in snow and high altitude. This unit was known as the 10th Mountain Division. It was key to several battles in Italy in 1945. Today a series of backcountry huts for recreation is named in honor of these soldiers.

## AGRICULTURE

Many Americans moved west to take advantage of the Homestead Act of 1862. This allowed any

US citizen to claim up to 160 acres (65 ha) of land free of cost. Once claimed, the person had to live on the land for at least five years, build a home on it, and farm it. Agriculture in the state got a boost from the mining industry in the mid-1800s. The arrival of mine workers increased demand for food grown by local farmers.

Farming and ranching proved difficult on Colorado's dry plains. However, irrigation was a game changer. Soon ditches and canals brought much-needed water to the industry. This helped crops such as hay, sugar beets, melons, grapes, grains, and more. Cattle and sheep ranching on the range also increased. This fostered a cowboy culture in the late 1800s that remains a part of Colorado today. In fact, when the new Denver football team played its first season in 1960, it was named the Broncos. A bronco is an untamed horse. The name for the National Football League (NFL) team is in honor of the state's ranching heritage. Cowboys relied on horses to move cattle. They sometimes trained broncos.

Some people enjoy white water rafting on the Colorado River.

Agriculture is still a main force in Colorado's economy and culture. The leading agricultural product is livestock. Dairy products, corn, and wheat are also important to Colorado's agriculture industry.

## TOURISM

Colorado's most important resources are its climate and scenery. People come from all over the world to see the mountains in all four seasons. People visit mountain towns in winter to ski on Colorado's powdery snow.

The park Garden of the Gods attracts many tourists. They admire its red rock formations.

In other seasons people may hike or bike. Others go rafting, fishing, or camping. Some just take in the views and enjoy the natural settings. There are also many natural hot springs in the state to relax in during any season.

All of this has led to a booming service industry that began in the 1800s. Colorado is now a popular state to visit. Tourism is a cornerstone of the state's economy. Businesses that provide services include hotels, restaurants, ski resorts, guest ranches, and more.

## FURTHER EVIDENCE

**Chapter Four discusses Colorado's climate and scenery. What evidence can you find in the book to support the main point of this chapter? The website below gives an in-depth look at one of the parks. What information at the website supports this point?**

### GARDEN OF THE GODS PARK

**abdocorelibrary.com/colorado**

20th Street ½
Park Ave 1
38th Ave
Junction I-70 1½

CHAPTER FIVE

# PEOPLE AND PLACES

The people of Colorado are known as Coloradans. The population is nearly 5.8 million. Almost 5 million of those residents live on the Front Range. People who are white and are not Hispanic or Latino make up 67.7 percent of the population. Hispanic or Latino Coloradans make up 21.8 percent of the population. Black people are 4.6 percent, and Asians are 3.5 percent. Today American Indians are 1.6 percent of the population.

Denver is the largest city in Colorado.

## PERSPECTIVES

### A GREAT PLACE TO LIVE

**Colorado is often high on the lists of places that provide an excellent quality of life. There are urban areas with easy access to arts, music, culture, science, and professional sports. There is an international airport in Denver. The state also has a thriving business sector. And yet so much of the state is wilderness. There are endless opportunities for nature lovers. The *US News & World Report* named Boulder the top place to live in 2020. One resident said, "This [town] attracts young professionals, families, academics, scientists, transplants from both coasts . . . and, above all, lovers of outdoor recreation."**

Colorado is growing. Its cities are often ranked as some of the best places in the nation to live. Boulder, Denver, Fort Collins, and Colorado Springs were all in the top five of the *US News & World Report* listing of the best places to live in the country from 2020 to 2021.

Famous Coloradans include Clara Brown, who was freed from slavery in 1856 and moved to Colorado in 1859. In the mining town of Central City, she soon became a successful businesswoman. John Denver was a popular musician. He spent time in the state and lived there for several years as an adult. He wrote many songs about its beauty, including "Rocky Mountain High." NFL quarterback John Elway led the Denver Broncos to win two Super Bowls. Several Olympic skiers are also from Colorado, including Mikaela Shiffrin, Buddy Werner, and Jeremy Bloom.

### PARKS IN COLORADO

**In addition to Rocky Mountain National Park, Colorado has 3 other national parks and 42 state parks. One of the national parks is the Great Sand Dunes National Park and Preserve. This park includes 30 square miles (78 sq km) of dunes nestled against the Sangre de Cristo Mountains. Mesa Verde National Park preserves the relics of Ancestral Pueblo people in the southwest corner of the state. And the Black Canyon of Gunnison National Park features steep, dramatic cliffs carved by the Gunnison River.**

## PLACES

There are many mountain towns in Colorado with

recreation opportunities. Estes Park is at the east entrance to Rocky Mountain National Park. Steamboat Springs, Ouray, and Leadville are other mountain towns in the state. Colorado also has some of the country's best skiing in towns such as Winter Park, Aspen, and Durango.

Many people also visit Denver, the largest city in the state. Its nickname is the Mile High City because its elevation is 1 mile (1.6 km) above sea level. The city offers museums, theaters, bike paths, restaurants, and sports arenas. Many of Colorado's professional sports teams call Denver home. They include football's Denver Broncos, baseball's Colorado Rockies, basketball's Denver Nuggets, soccer's Colorado Rapids, and hockey's Colorado Avalanche.

There are also rodeos, county fairs, and other events that feature the cowboy culture in Colorado. The National Western Stock Show is one national event.

**Coloradans love to cheer on their favorite teams, including the Colorado Avalanche.**

The National Western Stock Show features events including saddle bronc riding.

It was established in 1906 and is held every January for more than two weeks. The show celebrates farming and ranching.

In the summertime Colorado also hosts numerous music festivals. The Telluride Bluegrass Festival happens in Telluride, and the RockyGrass Festival takes place in Lyons. One other famous festival in Colorado is the Crested Butte Wildflower Festival. This festival occurs every summer at the peak of wildflower season. From city exploration to adventures in nature, there's much to see and do in Colorado.

# STRAIGHT TO THE SOURCE

Beginning in the early 1900s, the land of Staunton State Park was homesteaded by the Staunton family. When Frances Hornbrook Staunton died in 1986, the land was donated to the state according to her will, which said:

> *Said land . . . is given to the State of Colorado for use as a State Park to be known as "Staunton State Park," and to be preserved essentially as a wilderness area. It is my further intention that . . . this property be preserved . . . for public benefit as a natural wilderness-type park.*
>
> *At least ninety percent (90%) of the area is to be left in its natural state with only those modifications by man which are necessary to preserve the area in its natural state, typifying Colorado's most beautiful mountain forest and meadow region.*

Source: *Francis Staunton's Will, Staunton State Park: Final Master Plan*. Colorado State Parks, Winter 2010, cpw.state.co.us. PDF. Accessed 23 Aug. 2021.

## CONSIDER YOUR AUDIENCE

Adapt this passage for a different audience, such as your younger friends. Write a blog post conveying this same information for the new audience. How does your post differ from the original text and why?

# IMPORTANT DATES

**10,000 years ago**
Paleo-Indians live on the land that is now Colorado.

**500s CE**
Ancestral Puebloans establish settlements and a culture in the Mesa Verde area.

**1598**
The Spanish claim most of western Colorado.

**1682**
Robert de La Salle claims the eastern part of Colorado for France. Colorado becomes part of the Louisiana Territory.

**1803**
The US government acquires the eastern part of Colorado as part of the Louisiana Purchase.

**1848**
The United States gains control of the western half of Colorado at the end of the Mexican-American War.

**1861**
Colorado becomes a US territory.

**1864**
Colorado Cavalry troops kill approximately 200 peaceful Cheyenne and Arapaho people in the Sand Creek Massacre.

**1876**
Colorado gains statehood 100 years after the signing of the Declaration of Independence, resulting in the nickname the Centennial State.

**1960**
The Denver Broncos football team plays its first season.

# STOP AND THINK

## Say What?

Studying a state can mean learning a lot of new vocabulary. Find five words in this book you've never heard before. Use a dictionary to find out what they mean. Then write the meanings in your own words and use each word in a new sentence.

## Dig Deeper

After reading this book, what questions do you still have about Colorado? With an adult's help, find a few reliable sources that can help you answer your questions. Write a paragraph about what you learned.

## Tell the Tale

Chapter One of this book reveals the beauty of Colorado and its diversity of scenery. Imagine you are driving through the state. Write 200 words about everything you see and do. What is your favorite part of the trip?

## Take a Stand

Coloradans think their state is a great place to live and visit. There are outdoor activities to do year-round. The scenery is diverse and breathtaking, and wildlife is abundant. If someone could visit only one place in Colorado, which do you think would be the best place to see? Why?

# GLOSSARY

**amend**
to modify something in order to improve it

**boom**
a period of quick growth

**bust**
a business failure

**constitution**
a document laying out the basic beliefs and laws of a nation or state

**elevation**
the height above sea level

**headwaters**
the source of a river or stream

**homestead**
land given by the US government that becomes personal property after a person takes care of it for some years

**irrigation**
the process of watering crops though human-made means, such as pipes

**mesa**
a wide, elevated area of land that is relatively flat at the top

**plateau**
high, flat land

**urban**
relating to a city environment

# ONLINE RESOURCES

To learn more about Colorado, visit our free resource websites below.

**Core Library CONNECTION**
FREE! COMMON CORE MULTIMEDIA RESOURCES

Visit **abdocorelibrary.com** or scan this QR code for free Common Core resources for teachers and students, including vetted activities, multimedia, and booklinks, for deeper subject comprehension.

**Booklinks NONFICTION NETWORK**
FREE! ONLINE NONFICTION RESOURCES

Visit **abdobooklinks.com** or scan this QR code for free additional online weblinks for further learning. These links are routinely monitored and updated to provide the most current information available.

# LEARN MORE

Cooper, Robert. *Denver Broncos.* Abdo, 2020.

Tekiela, Stan. *The Kids' Guide to Birds of Colorado.* Adventure, 2021.

Yasuda, Anita. *Exploring the West.* Abdo, 2018.

# INDEX



## About the Author

Laura Perdew is a mom, writing consultant, and author of more than 40 books for children. She writes both fiction and nonfiction with a focus on nature, the environment, and environmental issues. Laura herself is a Coloradan and enjoys hiking, camping, and everything the state has to offer.